Pebble® Plus

Famous Firsts

THE FIRST SPACE MISSIONS

by Megan Cooley Peterson

Consulting Editor: Gail Saunders-Smith, PhD

Consultant: Jonson Miller, PhD
Associate Teaching Professor of History and Science,
Technology, and Society
Drexel University

CAPSTONE PRESS
a capstone imprint

Pebble Plus is published by Capstone Press,
1710 Roe Crest Drive, North Mankato, Minnesota 56003
www.capstonepub.com

Library of Congress Cataloging-in-Publication Data
Peterson, Megan Cooley.
 The first space missions / Megan Cooley Peterson.
    pages cm.—(Famous firsts)
 Includes bibliographical references and index.
 ISBN 978-1-4914-0576-5 (hb)—ISBN 978-1-4914-0644-1 (pb)—ISBN 978-1-4914-0610-6 (eb)
1. Outer space—Exploration—Juvenile literature. 2. Manned space flight—Juvenile literature. I. Title.
 TL793.P4845 2015
 629.4'1—dc23   2014001803

Editorial Credits
Erika L. Shores, editor; Terri Poburka, designer; Svetlana Zhurkin, media researcher; Laura Manthe, production specialist

Photo Credits
AP Photo: Sovfoto, 19; Getty Images: Gamma-Keystone, 7; NASA, cover, 5, 15, 21; Newscom: akg-images/RIA Nowosti, 9,
11, ITAR-TASS, 17 (inset), Universal Images Group/Sovfoto, 13; Shutterstock: July Flower, 17

Note to Parents and Teachers

The Famous Firsts set supports national social studies standards related to science, technology,
and society. This book describes and illustrates the first space missions. The images support early
readers in understanding the text. The repetition of words and phrases helps early readers learn
new words. This book also introduces early readers to subject-specific vocabulary words, which are
defined in the Glossary section. Early readers may need assistance to read some words and to use
the Table of Contents, Glossary, Read More, Internet Sites, Critical Thinking Using the Common
Core, and Index sections of the book.

Printed in the United States of America in North Mankato, Minnesota.
032014   008087CGF14

Table of Contents

Space Travel

Blast off! Spacecraft zoom
among the stars. They go on
missions to learn about space.
Climb aboard some of
the first space missions.

Animals in Space

Animals went on early missions. They made sure space was safe for people. Albert II was the first monkey in space.

The United States sends Albert II to space.

1949

A monkey named Sam flew in space 11 years after Albert II.

Satellites

The space-age began when *Sputnik 1* shot into space. This satellite circled Earth once every 96 minutes. It sent information back to Earth.

The United States sends Albert II to space.

1949

1957

Russia launches the first satellite into space.

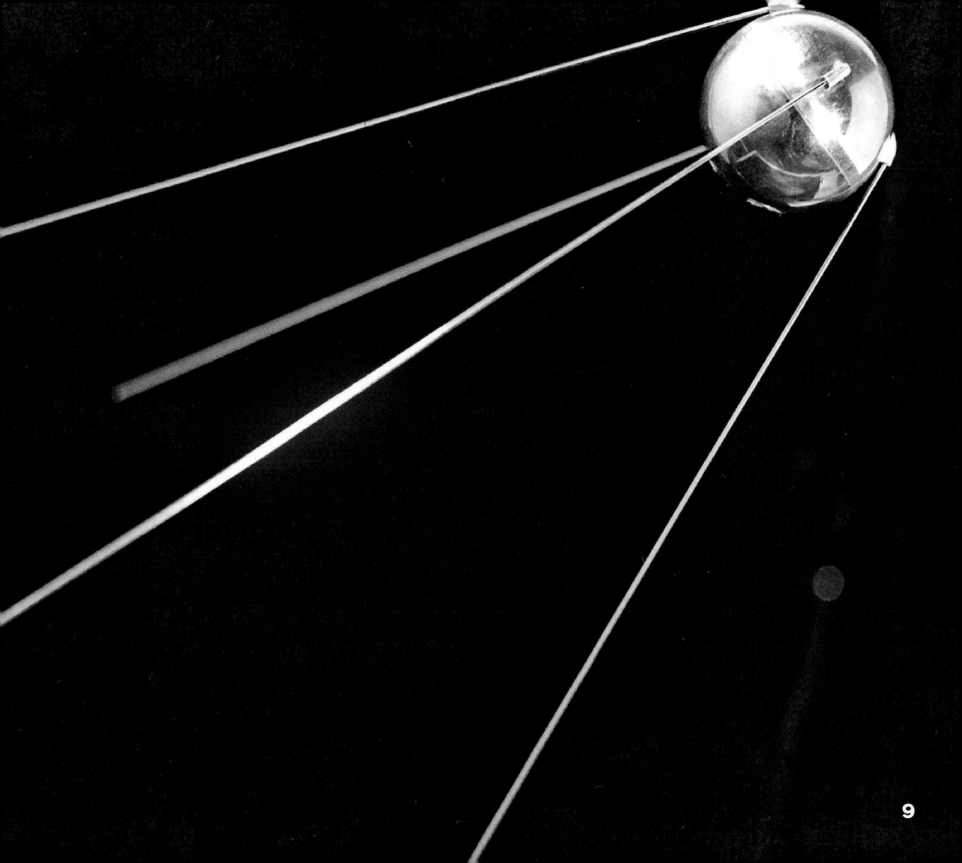

Humans in Space

Yuri Gagarin made history as the first human in space. He circled Earth one time in *Vostok 1*. His trip lasted 1.5 hours.

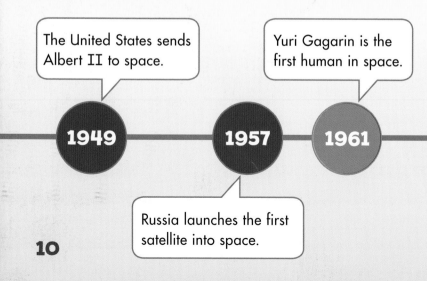

The United States sends Albert II to space.

Yuri Gagarin is the first human in space.

1949

1957

1961

Russia launches the first satellite into space.

Women in Space

The first woman in space took an even longer flight. Valentina Tereshkova circled Earth 48 times in *Vostok 6.* She was in space for almost three days.

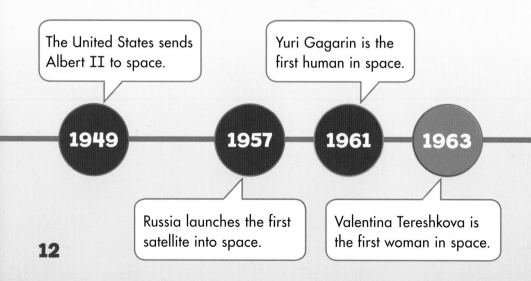

The United States sends Albert II to space.

Yuri Gagarin is the first human in space.

1949

1957

1961

1963

Russia launches the first satellite into space.

Valentina Tereshkova is the first woman in space.

Moon Landing

Neil Armstrong put his boot

into the moon's dust.

Buzz Aldrin followed.

They had just become the first

people to walk on the moon.

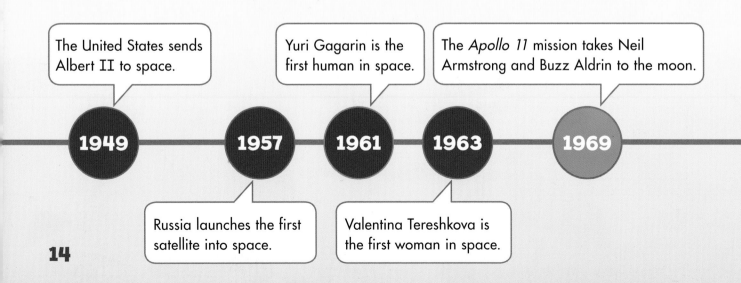

The United States sends Albert II to space.

Yuri Gagarin is the first human in space.

The *Apollo 11* mission takes Neil Armstrong and Buzz Aldrin to the moon.

1949 **1957** **1961** **1963** **1969**

Russia launches the first satellite into space.

Valentina Tereshkova is the first woman in space.

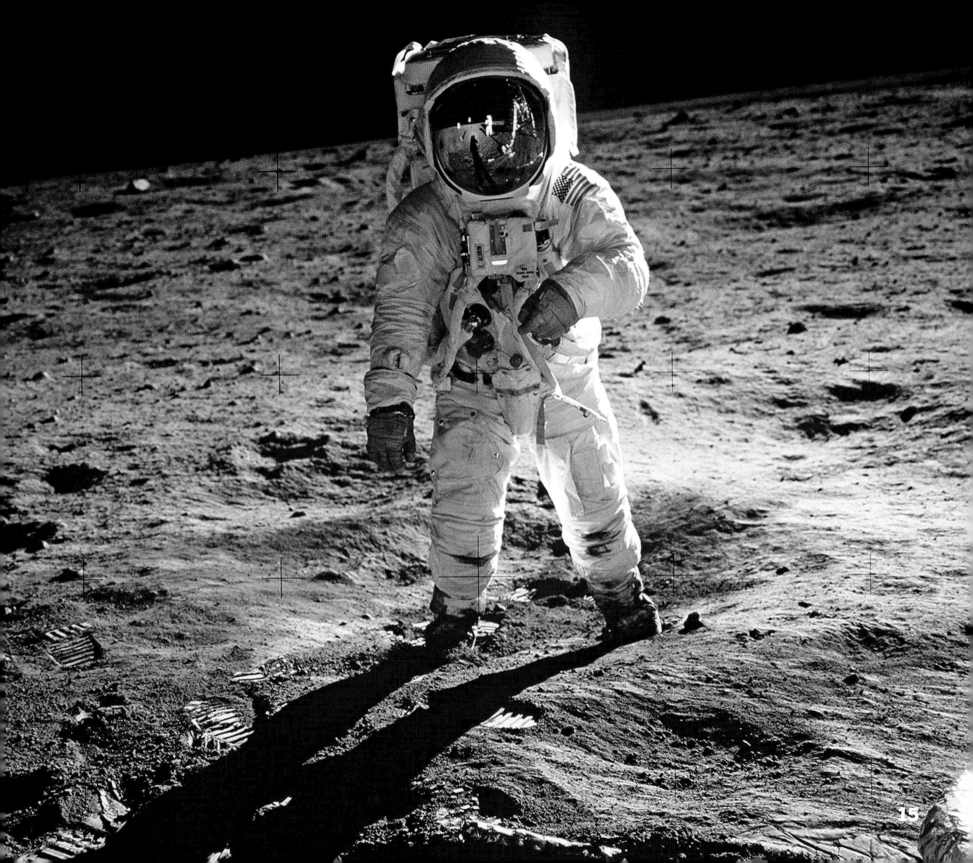

Space Probes

Venera 7 was the first space probe to land on Venus. The probe measured Venus's temperature at 887 degrees Fahrenheit (475 degrees Celsius).

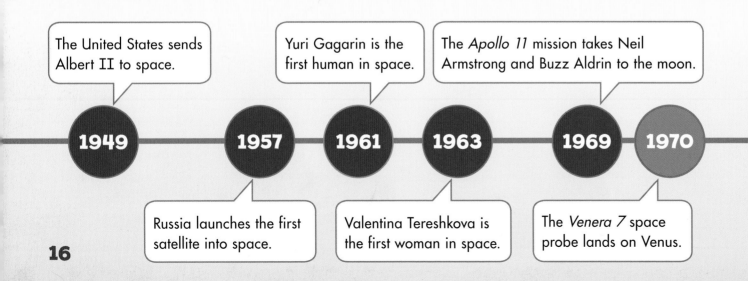

The United States sends Albert II to space.

Yuri Gagarin is the first human in space.

The *Apollo 11* mission takes Neil Armstrong and Buzz Aldrin to the moon.

1949 1957 1961 1963 1969 1970

Russia launches the first satellite into space.

Valentina Tereshkova is the first woman in space.

The *Venera 7* space probe lands on Venus.

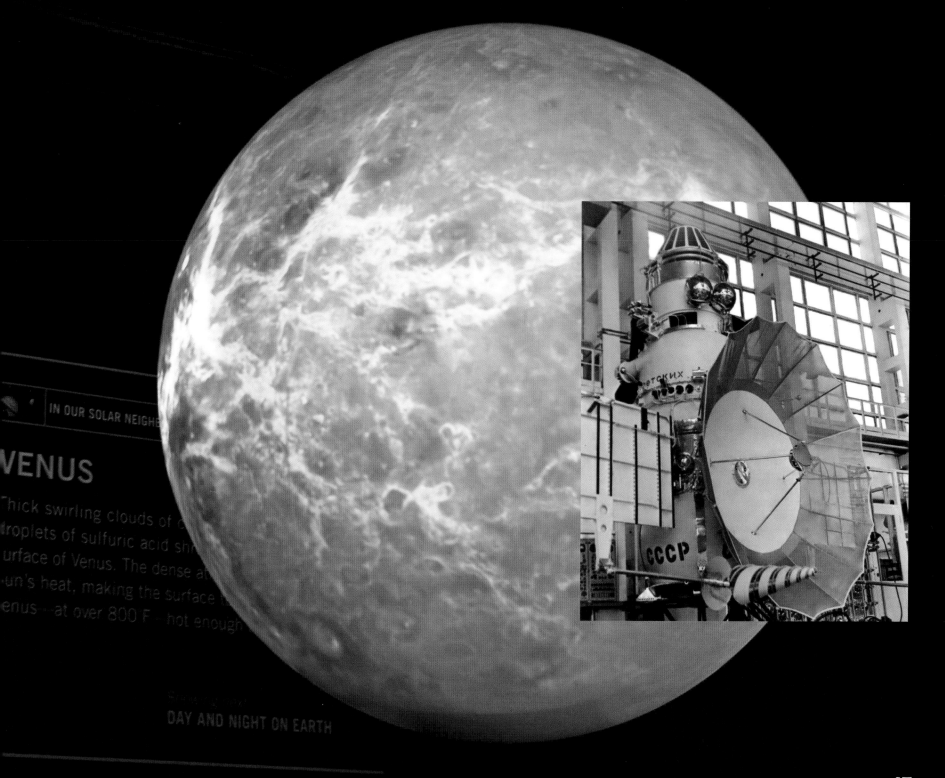

VENUS

Thick swirling clouds of c
droplets of sulfuric acid shr
surface of Venus. The dense a
un's heat, making the surface
enus—at over 800 F—hot enough

DAY AND NIGHT ON EARTH

Space Stations

Some astronauts live and work in space stations. The *Salyut 1* was the first space station. It circled Earth for 175 days.

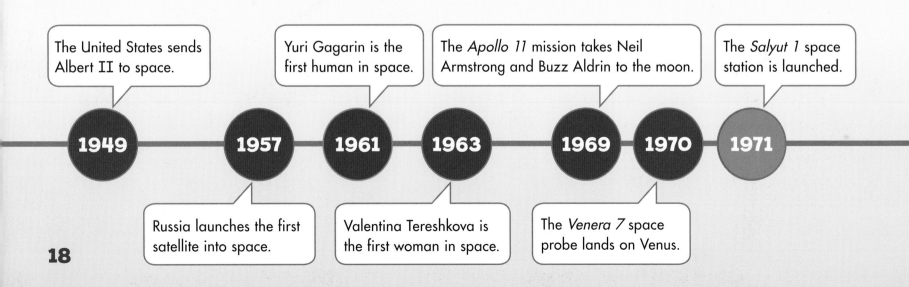

The United States sends Albert II to space.

Yuri Gagarin is the first human in space.

The *Apollo 11* mission takes Neil Armstrong and Buzz Aldrin to the moon.

The *Salyut 1* space station is launched.

1949   1957   1961   1963   1969   1970   1971

Russia launches the first satellite into space.

Valentina Tereshkova is the first woman in space.

The *Venera 7* space probe lands on Venus.

Space Shuttles

Space shuttles flew astronauts into space for 30 years. NASA's *Columbia* was the first space shuttle. The final shuttle flew in 2011.

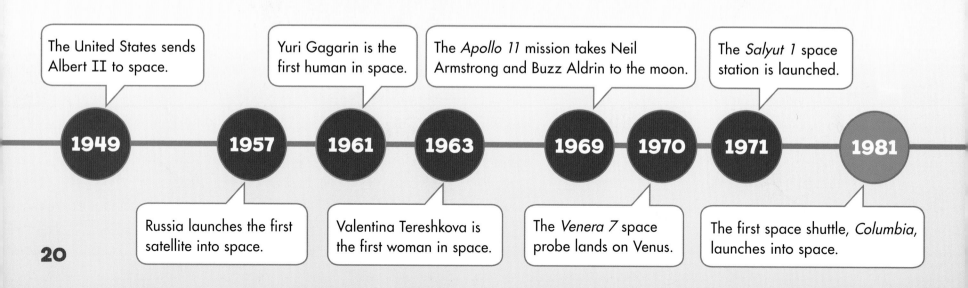

The United States sends Albert II to space.

Yuri Gagarin is the first human in space.

The *Apollo 11* mission takes Neil Armstrong and Buzz Aldrin to the moon.

The *Salyut 1* space station is launched.

1949   **1957**   **1961**   **1963**   **1969**   **1970**   **1971**   **1981**

Russia launches the first satellite into space.

Valentina Tereshkova is the first woman in space.

The *Venera 7* space probe lands on Venus.

The first space shuttle, *Columbia*, launches into space.

Glossary

astronaut—a person who is trained to live and work in space

NASA—a U.S. government agency that does research on flight and space exploration; NASA stands for National Aeronautics and Space Administration

probe—a tool or device used to study or explore something

satellite—a spacecraft that circles Earth; satellites gather and send information

space-age—the period of time when space exploration first became possible

space shuttle—a spacecraft that is meant to carry astronauts into space and back to Earth

space station—a spacecraft that circles Earth; astronauts can live on space stations for long periods of time

Read More

Conrad, David. *Exploring Space.* Earth and Space Science. Mankato, Minn.: Capstone Press, 2012.

Kortenkamp, Steve. *Show Me Space: My First Picture Encyclopedia.* My First Picture Encyclopedias. Mankato, Minn.: Capstone Press, 2013.

Peters, Elisa. *Outer Space.* PowerKids Readers: The Universe. New York: PowerKids Press, 2013.

Internet Sites

FactHound offers a safe, fun way to find Internet sites related to this book. All of the sites on FactHound have been researched by our staff.

Here's all you do:

Visit *www.facthound.com*

Type in this code: 9781491405765

Super-cool stuff!

Check out projects, games and lots more at
www.capstonekids.com

23

Critical Thinking Using the Common Core

1. Why do you think animals went into space before people? (Integration of Knowledge and Ideas)

2. What makes a space station different from other spacecraft? (Key Ideas and Details)

Index

Word Count: 208
Grade: 1
Early-Intervention Level: 19